Robert K. Douglas

The Language and Literature of China

Two Lectures Delivered at the Royal Institution of Great Britain

Robert K. Douglas

The Language and Literature of China
Two Lectures Delivered at the Royal Institution of Great Britain

ISBN/EAN: 9783337071660

Printed in Europe, USA, Canada, Australia, Japan

Cover: Foto ©Thomas Meinert / pixelio.de

More available books at **www.hansebooks.com**

THE

LANGUAGE AND LITERATURE OF CHINA.

TWO LECTURES

DELIVERED AT THE

ROYAL INSTITUTION OF GREAT BRITAIN

IN

MAY AND JUNE, 1875.

BY

ROBERT K. DOUGLAS,

OF THE BRITISH MUSEUM, AND PROFESSOR OF CHINESE AT
KING'S COLLEGE, LONDON.

LONDON:

TRÜBNER & CO., 57 AND 59, LUDGATE HILL.

1875.

LECTURE I.

THE LANGUAGE OF CHINA.

THE course of recent events in China indicates with sufficient plainness that the " Middle Kingdom " cannot much longer maintain the isolation in which she has wrapt herself for so many centuries. The advances which have of late years been made by our diplomatists, our missionaries, and our merchants, in influencing the opinions of those classes of the people with which they are brought into contact; the increased facilities of communication between the East and West afforded by steam and electricity; and the rapid—perhaps too rapid—strides with which her enterprising neighbour Japan is hastening forward in the march of

modern civilization ;—are all urging her with a
pressure which she cannot successfully resist,
strive as much as she may, into the fellowship
of those western nations whose friendly overtures
she has up to this time treated with unfeigned
indifference and contempt.

That she should have succeeded in separating
herself for so long from the rest of the world is
doubtless due in a great measure to the geographical position of the country. Bounded
on the east by the sea, on the west by vast
sandy wastes, on the south and south-west by
mountainous districts for the most part inhabited
by tribes whom it is usual to describe as virtu-
ally independent and half savage, and on the
north by range after range of mountains rising
like sharks' teeth from the plain, and dwarfing
into insignificance the " Great Wall " which
remains a monument of the folly as well as
of the industry of the Chinese race, she has
dwelt, like Laish of old, quiet and secure ; while
at the same time the varied extent and richness
of her internal resources has enabled her, without
seeking the natural or artificial products of other

countries, to supply her people with enough and to spare of all the necessaries of life. Independent then of all the world, beyond comparison more powerful, by reason of her wealth, her size, and the nature of her inhabitants, than any of her neighbours—a very Triton among minnows, admitting no rivals, and courting no alliances, she stood, and was content to stand, alone. Accepting nothing from the world beyond her own frontiers in religion, literature, science, or art, which did not fall in with the national views on those subjects, and which she could not make her own, receiving no impress from without, and rejecting peremptorily everything thrown in her way which was distasteful to her, she brooded over the east of Asia, absorbing only that which assimilated easily with the national tastes and the preconceived ideas of the people.

Thus, though in the course of the history of China tribes from other parts of Asia have, by force of arms, successfully invaded the country, and have entered in and taken possession, their advent has in no wise affected the national life, and when they have yielded

their powers to others, they have left no
more distinctive trace behind them than do
mountain torrents when they lose themselves in
the ocean. A modern instance in point is the
fact, as has been lately remarked, that at Canton
and other large cities in China, the imperial
Tatar garrisons have been completely absorbed
into the native population. But it may possibly
be said that at least the Chinese of the first
century accepted and adopted from India the
religion of Buddha. True, they did ; but, like
the Manchu and Mongolian invaders, it had, if
I may so say, to go through the process of
digestion and assimilation. It was forced into
a like mould to those from which had issued
forth the national religions of Confucianism and
Taouism and the result has been that practically
—of course much of the literature still remains
Indian—it is difficult to recognize in the beliefs
of modern Chinese Buddhists anything more
than traces of the pure and lofty teachings of
Sakyamuni. But the introduction of Buddhism
from India brought to the notice of the Chinese
of that day something more than the religious

system of its founder. It forced on their
attention a comparison between the alphabetical
system of writing as existing in Sanskrit and
their own unwieldy characters. But neither
then, nor at a still earlier period, when their
armies marched across Central and Western
Asia to the borders of the Caspian Sea, did
their acquaintance with the more simple mode
of expressing thoughts on paper, employed by
the people of some of the countries through
which they passed, ever shake their faith for a
moment in their native symbols.

It is true that the adoption of an alphabetical
system of writing would have revolutionized the
language, and that as it then stood, and as it now
stands, it would be impossible to express it, for
general purposes, in any other way than through
the medium of the written character then as now
existing. But no thought of suggesting the possibility of such a change, which, though attended
with immediate inconvenience, would have re-
sulted in infinite advantage, appears to have
occurred to any writer or statesman of that day.
The nearest approach to it was the adoption of

a system of syllabic spelling for the purposes
at first of representing the sounds of Indian
and other foreign names in the native character,
and later of spelling as it were the sounds of
characters in the native dictionaries, but beyond
this its application has not been extended.) For
Chinese scholars it was sufficient to know that
their written characters " embalmed the wisdom
and reflected the sagacity of ages." In them
Confucius gave vent to his musings, and in
them the followers of the sage had stereotyped
his sayings and his doings; and like as devout
Mahommedans would scorn the notion of transcribing the Koran into any language but that
in which Mahommed wrote, so have Chinamen
through all ages clung to the form of written
character used by Confucius as the only channel
through which his ineffable wisdom should be
transmitted to future ages. Thus the written
character has remained unchanged, and is, from
a Chinaman's point of view, unchangeable.

But while the Chinese have shown themselves
thus supremely indifferent to all the world in
general, its arts, its sciences, its opinions, and

its friendships, an almost equal degree of apathy has been displayed by Englishmen concerning everything connected with China except her trade. A language which is the language of 400,000,000 of our fellow-men, and a literature which goes back to the time of King David, and which found its fullest development before these shores were invaded by the Norman conquerors, have been passed by as though they possessed no sort of interest to us who yearly exchange merchandise to the amount of £40,000,000 sterling with the men whose speech we ignore and whose learning we treat as though it were beneath our notice. Our stake in China is larger than that of any other European country, and yet, as far as the diffusion of a knowledge of the language is concerned, we are behind both France and Russia. And with the exception of two or three scholars, among whom Dr. Birch of the British Museum, and Mr. Beal, the learned translator of several works on Chinese Buddhism, are chief, the study of Chinese has been with us entirely confined to those who by the nature of their professional duties are compelled to grapple with the language. On the other hand, France, who, as a French consul once said to me, brings to China her ideas, while England imports her merchandise, can present a long list of Sinologues, among whom the well-known names of Julien, Klaproth, Remusat and Pauthier claim the pre-eminence, who never trod the soil of China, but who, having devoted themselves to the study of Chinese from a true scholarly instinct, have left behind them for our benefit a rich inheritance of knowledge. At the present time there are three Professorial Chairs of Chinese in Paris, and a goodly array of students attend each lecture room. In London there are two chairs, one of which has been empty for some time, and which when filled disappointed its founders by leaving its occupant undisturbed in the enjoyment of the full disposal of his time. As yet Chinese has been entirely unrepresented at both Oxford and Cambridge; but I am glad to be able to state that lately a movement has been set on foot, through the energy of Sir Rutherford Alcock and others, for the establishment of a Chinese

Professorship at the older University. And all those who are interested in the study of the language will be glad to know that, should the scheme be carried into effect, Dr. Legge, the well-known translator of the Chinese classics, will probably be the first holder of the office.

No doubt the difficulties, or the supposed difficulties of acquiring a knowledge of the language, have prevented many English scholars from taking the grammar and dictionary in hand. But I think that, with your leave, I shall be able to show that these difficulties have been much overrated. Stanislas Julien began the study of Chinese in Paris in the year 1823, and in 1825 he published an excellent translation in Latin of the philosophical works of Mencius, which is certainly not one of the easiest books in the language; and to any one who will bring an equal amount of absorbing energy to the work, the fortified places of Chinese will surely yield, though not perhaps as easily as they did to one who from the first gained for himself a foremost place in the front rank of European Sinologues.

What then is the Chinese language? It is the
chief among that small class of languages which
includes the Thibetan, Cochin-Chinese, Burmese,
Corean and Chinese, and which is usually
described as monosyllabic. (It is language in
its most archaic form. Every word is a root,
and every root is a word. It is without
inflexion or even agglutination; its substantives are indeclinable, and its verbs are not to
be conjugated; it is destitute of an alphabet,
and finds its expression on paper in thousands
of distinct symbols.)

No wonder then that it has been a cause
of surprise and perplexity to many. "In a
country," says one writer, "where the roses
have no fragrance, and the women no petti-
coats; where the labourer has no Sabbath,
and the magistrate no sense of honour; where
the roads bear no vehicles, and the ships no
keels; where the needle points to the south,
and the sign of being puzzled is to scratch
the antipodes of the head; where the place
of honour is on the left hand, and the seat
of intellect is in the stomach; where to take

off your hat is an insolent gesture, and to wear white garments is to put yourself into mourning—we ought not to be astonished to find a literature without an alphabet, and a language without a grammar."

"Here then," writes another author, "is the most primitive language, and the one therefore from which all others have sprung." Since these last words were written some decades have passed, and further research has not definitely confirmed their truth. No doubt a language possessing such characteristics as I have mentioned affords a tempting field for the comparative philologist. Here is a language of monosyllabic roots, which, as regards the written character, has been checked in its growth and crystallized in its most ancient form by the early occurrence of a period of great literary activity, of which the nation is proud, and to the productions of which every Chinaman even of the present day looks back as containing the true standards of literary excellence. If then from a language such as Sanskrit, with its overgrowth of agglutinations

and inflexions, such great results, as have of
late years been made known, can be obtained,
what may not be expected from a language
in so simple a form as Chinese? Such an
expectation is reasonable, and we may antici-
pate that philology will be a great gainer by an
extended knowledge of it. But as yet we are
not sufficiently acquainted with its various spoken
forms. It requires as it were kneading and pre-
paring before it can be used as a weapon by
the comparative philologist, and as a first step
it is necessary that we should trace back the
sounds to their original forms. But the difficulty which meets us here is, that unlike the
languages of the West, there is no inherent connexion between the sounds and the written
medium; thus a character which is called to-
day *chi*, was called a couple of thousand years
ago *'tek*, and equally wide variations in pro-
nunciation are observable in all the dialects
which are spoken at the present day. Investigation also has proved that in no one of these
dialects is the language pronounced as formerly,
and the result is, that only by a careful

comparison of the dialects with the ancient rhythmical writings, and the syllabic spelling based on the Sanskrit alphabet which was introduced with the knowledge of Buddhism from India, as well as by tracing the sounds of the characters as preserved in Japan and the neighbouring countries, can we hope to arrive at a certain knowledge of the ancient sounds of the language. Considerable progress has already been made by Mr. Edkins in this direction. We now know, thanks to his labours, in what part of the Empire to look for the old finals *m, k, t, p,* which have long been lost in most of the provinces, and where we may expect to find the initials *d, b, z, dz, zh,* still playing the same part in the spoken language that they did in the time of Confucius; and it is only by thus tracing back the sounds to their most ancient forms that we can compare it, with a reasonable prospect of success, with other languages.

But these studies refer more especially to the sounds of the language; and in treating of the two branches into which Chinese naturally

divides itself, namely, the written medium or
characters, and the spoken medium or sounds,
I propose to begin with the former. And in
following this course I shall be doing no violence to the language, for it would be quite
possible to separate the characters from the
sounds, and to treat them as two languages, as
indeed has already been partly done in Japan,
where the Chinese characters were at one time
in general use as representing the phonetic value
of their Japanese equivalents. Beginning at the
other end, but with a similar ultimate result,
various members of the missionary body have
published text books and dictionaries in Roman-
ized Chinese, that is to say, they have avoided
the use of the characters by transcribing the
sounds of the language in Roman letters. But
since, though the characters are rich and copious
to a degree, the sounds are out of all proportion·
poor, this last dismemberment presents the language in a very denuded form, and is at the same
time attended with difficulties which only the
most sanguine can hope to see overcome. The
necessity of distinguishing between words having

the same sound can only be met by the adoption of distinct diacritical marks for each word ; and as one sound often represents as many as a hundred words, such a system cannot be unattended with confusion.

The characters of the language form the medium which speaks to the eye, and may be described as the equivalents of the written *words* of other languages ; but unlike these, instead of being composed of letters of an alphabet, they are either symbols intended to represent images, or are formed by a combination of lines, or of two or more such symbols. All characters, say the Chinese lexicographers, had their origin in single strokes, or in hieroglyphics, and this no doubt is a correct view of the case. Legends differ as to who was the first inventor of writing in China. One attributes the invention to Fuh-he (3200 B.C.), who is also said to have instituted marriage, and to have introduced the use of clothing, and who caused the knotted cords, which had been up to that time in use, to be superseded by characters founded on the shapes of his celebrated diagrams. Another record states that Tsang Ke, who lived B.C. 2700, was the Cadmus of China. According to received native accounts, Tsang Ke was a man of extraordinary ability, and was acquainted with the art of writing from his birth. While wandering in the neighbourhood of his house at Yang-woo, he one day met with a tortoise, and observing its shell distinctly and beautifully spotted, he took it home, and thus formed the idea of representing the objects around him. Looking upwards, he carefully observed the figures presented by the stars and the heavenly bodies; he then attentively considered the forms of birds, and of mountains and rivers, etc., and from them at length originated the written character.

But however great the uncertainty may be as to who invented the first characters, we may take it for granted that they were simply pictures of the various objects of sense which were present to the eye of the writer. Thus when he wished to express a mountain, he wrote, as did also the ancient Egyptians, $\triangle\!\!\triangle$, a symbol which is written at the present day 山 ;) now written 月, served him to signify the moon, and so on. But such a written medium was naturally extremely limited, and by degrees, in some instances, by the addition of strokes, and in others by a combination of one or more of these primary characters, the written language has been formed as it is at the present day.   In tracing the growth of the later characters we are assisted by the native philologists, who have divided them into six classes.

The first they call *Siang hing*, lit. characters representing the forms of the objects meant, or, as we should say, Hieroglyphics, such as those thus mentioned, and about 600 more, as, for example, ⊙ *jih* 'the sun;' 馬 *ma* 'a horse,' etc.; and of these are composed, with a few exceptions, the 214 determinative or radical characters, one of which enters into the composition of every character in the language.

The second class is called *Chi ooo*, lit. characters indicating things, that is to say, characters intended to represent ideas to the mind by the position of their parts. Thus the character

2

⊙ *tan* 'dawn,' in which the sun is represented as appearing above the horizon, belongs to it, and also such characters as 上 *shang* 'above,' and 下 *hea* 'beneath,' which are formed, in the one case, by placing a man above the medium level, and in the other below it.

The third class is made up of *Hwuy i*, lit. characters combining ideas, or Ideographics. This class is formed by uniting two or more significant characters to give the idea of a third. Of the time when these characters were invented we know nothing; but it is plain that their introduction must have given a very extended scope to the language, and they offer an interesting study, as, in many instances, giving us an insight into the moral and social conditions of those who framed them. For instance, if we analyze the character 信 *sin* 'sincere,' we find that it is formed by the combination of the characters 人 *jin* 'a man,' and 言 *yen* 'words,' a collocation of ideas which speaks well for the honourable truthfulness of the ancient Chinese, and which, when the unfortunate failing in this respect of their descendants is borne in mind, is decidedly opposed to the Darwinian theory as applied to language. The character 皇 *Hwang* 'Emperor,' is another belonging to this class, which gives anything but a contemptible notion of the moral standard of the people. This symbol was originally written thus 皇, and was composed of the characters meaning 'oneself' and 'ruler;' the Emperor was therefore to be ruler of himself, or Autocrat in the true sense of the term; for how can a man, said the ancient sages, rule others unless he first learn to be master of himself?

Curiously enough, by the omission of a stroke, this character has assumed its present corrupted form, which consists of parts signifying 'white' and 'ruler,' and this, as was mentioned in a recent letter from the St. Petersburg Correspondent of the "Times," has been literally translated by the Mongols into Tchagau Khan, and then by the Russians into Biely Tsar, or White Tsar, the name by which the Emperor of Russia is now known throughout all Asia.

Another character in this class is 明 *ming* 'brightness,' which is composed of a com-

bination of the sun and moon to indicate
brilliancy. Altogether, of these Ideographics
there are said to be about 700 in the language,
although some writers have held that this class
is a very much larger one, and have justified
their belief by analyses which, to say the least,
are far-fetched. Callery quotes a Jesuit work,
in which it is stated that the character 船
chuen ‘a ship,’ contains to the eye of faith—
and we should imagine to that eye alone—a
reference to the Flood, since it consists of 舟
chow ‘a ship,’ 八 *pă* ‘eight,’ and 口 *kow* ‘a
mouth,’ plainly pointing, adds the writer, to
Noah’s ark with its eight inhabitants; and that
婪 *lan* ‘to covet and desire,’ bears traces of
Eve’s guilt in its component parts, which are
女 *neu* ‘a woman,’ and 木 *muh* ‘a tree,’ twice
repeated, illustrating the longing desire which
overcame our first parent when between the
trees of Life and of Good and Evil.

The fourth class is the *Chuen choo,* or characters which being inverted, either in form or
sound, assume different meanings. These number
about 372, and are formed in two ways: either

by some slight alteration of the character, as
the turning of a stroke or of strokes to the
left instead of the right, as, for instance, the
character for the hand pointing to the left in
this way 彐 means 'left,' and when turned thus
ナ, means 'right;' or by changing the sound
of the character, and with the sound the meaning. Of this kind are such characters as 樂,
which when pronounced *yŏ* means 'music,' and
when *lŏ*, 'delight,' and 易, which as *i* means
'easy,' and as *yĭh* means to 'change.'

The fifth class is the *Chia chieh*, lit. characters
having borrowed meanings, and consists of
about 600 characters, which are applied, as is
indicated by the name. of the division, in
a double sense, and hence have been called
Metaphorical. As an illustration of this class,
Chinese writers adduce the character 矢 *shi*
'an arrow,' which, from the straight course of
an arrow, has come to signify 'direct,' 'right,'
'a word spoken to the point.'

The sixth class, which is known as the *Chieh
shing*, or Phonetic, embraces over twenty thousand characters. The adoption of these Pho-

netics was the turning - point in the progress
of Chinese writing. As was the case with
the Egyptians, the Chinese found that, having
exhausted their power of invention in forming
hieroglyphics and ideographics, a further development of the characters was necessary;
and, like the subjects of the Pharaohs, they
adopted certain characters to represent certain
sounds. As to when or by whom this system
was inaugurated, whether it was introduced from
abroad, or whether it was the product of native
intelligence, history is silent; but when it was
once decided on, the language rapidly increased
and multiplied. "A character," writes a well-
known Chinese author, "is not sterile; once bound
to another, it gives birth to a son; and if this
be joined to another, a grandson is born, and
so on." The characters then which belong to the
class called Phonetic are composed of two parts,
namely, the Primitive or Phonetic element, that
is to say, one of the characters which have been
chosen to represent certain sounds, and which
gives the sound to the whole character, and
one of the 214 determinatives or radical characters of the language.

One or more of these determinatives enter into
the composition of every character in Chinese,
and as a very large proportion of them are
plainly hieroglyphics, they may be said to be
the foundation of the written language. As
might be expected from their nature as hieroglyphics, they include the most remarkable
objects of nature, such as the sun, moon, a
river, a mountain, fire, water, earth, wood,
stone, etc. ; the chief parts of the human
body, as the head, the heart, the hand, the
foot, the eye, the ear, etc.; the principal parts
of a house, as the roof, the door, etc.; domestic
animals, such as the sheep, the cow, the horse,
the dog, etc. ; the primary relations of society,
as father, mother, son, daughter, etc. ; qualities,
such as great, small, straight, crooked, high,
low, long, etc.; and actions, such as to see, to
speak, to walk, to run, to stop, to enter, to
follow, etc. They are thus admirably adapted
to form generic terms, and this is the part they
play in composition with the Primitives. For
instance, into the composition of every character
signifying anything made of wood, such as a

table, a chair, a club, etc., the determinative
character meaning 'wood' is introduced, and it
then serves much the same purpose as do the
words 'mat' and 'steam' in the compounds
'matshed' and 'steamboat.'

The number of the primitives has been
variously estimated. Dr. Marshman gives them
at 3867, Callery at about 1000, and later
writers have reckoned them to be from 1100
to 1200. Taking them even at the lowest of
these figures, it will readily be imagined how,
by combination with the 214 determinatives,
they may be made to form the thirty and odd
thousand distinct characters of the language,
since of course it would be possible by combining
each of the 1000 Primitives with every one of
the 214 Determinatives, to form more than seven
times that number of characters.

To illustrate this system of formation, I will
take the Primitive 我 *ngo* 'I,' which, by combination with 27 determinatives, produces as
many derivatives having the same phonetic
value, in this way—combined with the determinative 山 'a mountain,' it becomes 峨 *ngo*

'a high mountain;' with 女 *neu* 'a woman,' 娥 *ngo* 'fair,' 'beautiful;' with 艸 *tsao* 'grass,' 莪 *ngo* 'a certain herb;' with 鳥 *neaou* 'a bird,' 鵝 *ngo* 'a goose,' and so on. From these examples it will be observed that the determinatives play the part in some instances of adjectives; and in combination with their primitives they form an exact parallel with many Egyptian and Assyrian Ideophonetics. I have been favoured by Dr. Birch, of the British Museum, with the following example in Egyptian, showing precisely the same formation in the composition of the characters, and in the respective value of their parts, as is seen in the Chinese instance I have just referred to. 🐇 *Un* means in Egyptian 'a hare;' combined with this determinative ⊔ it becomes 🐇 *Un* 'to open;' and with this ⊙✕, 🐇⊙✕ *Un* 'an hour.' Speaking of Assyrian hieroglyphics, Sir Henry Rawlinson says, "Certain classes of words have a sign prefixed or suffixed to them, more commonly the former, by which their general character is indicated. The names of Gods, of men, of cities, of tribes, of wild animals, of domestic animals, of metals, of months, of the points of the compass, and of dignities are thus accompanied. The sign prefixed or suffixed may have originally represented a word; but when used in the way here spoken of, it is believed that it was not sounded, but served simply to indicate to the reader the sort of word which was placed before it."

By the kindness of Mr. George Smith I am enabled to illustrate Sir Henry Rawlinson's words by these examples. ⊱ means in Assyrian 'wood,' and is used as the determinative for things made of wood. Thus in combination with the Primitive ⊁ it becomes ⊱⊁ 'a sceptre;' and when combined with the Primitive ⟨⊰⟩ we have ⊱⟨⊰⟩ 'a bow.' Again, ⫫⊢ is used in the same way as the determinative for all carnivorous animals. As, for instance, ⫫⊢ ⟆ is 'a dog,' and ⫫⊢ ⊢⊱⫯ is 'a lion.' It will be seen that both the Egyptian and Assyrian characters here quoted are constructed on exactly the same principle as that to be

observed in the formation of the majority of
Chinese characters, but it is noticeable that in
Assyrian the Primitives do not retain in com-
position their phonetic values, as they generally
do in Chinese, and as they often do in
Egyptian.

Marking then the forces of the two parts of
the characters, we can easily imagine the way in
which new characters have from time to time
been formed. We will suppose, for instance, that
a tree for which a Chinaman wishes to give a
name on paper is known to him colloquially as
ma. The coiner of the new character would
then in the first place choose a common phonetic
or Primitive possessing the sound *ma*; very
possibly he would take the hieroglyphic 馬
ma 'a horse,' and would combine with it the
determinative 木 *muh*, meaning 'wood.' The
new character would then stand thus 樢, and
might be understood to signify 'the *ma*
tree;' but, unless previously informed, the reader
would be left in complete ignorance as to the sort
of tree meant, as the parts of the character would
only supply the information that it was either

a tree or something made of wood, and that
it was to be pronounced *ma*. This is equally
the case, speaking generally, with all the
characters. By a careful study of the phonetics it is possible to arrive at the sounds or
approximate sounds—for certain variations constantly occur—of the characters of the language;
but the only hint at their meanings is to be
derived from the determinatives, which point
only to the general nature of the objects or
actions signified.

As I have already said, the Determinatives
are 214 in number, and these have been
considered by many of the native dictionary-
makers to furnish convenient headings under
which to arrange the characters of the
language. Again, others have chosen to
classify the characters according to their final
sounds. Both systems have their advantages.
By adopting the first, the headings are comparatively few, and the characters are, roughly
speaking, classified according to the generic
meanings they have in common; and the second
gives constant practice to students in remem-

bering the tones and correct rhyming pronun-
ciation of the characters. But in both the
phonetic relationship between the Primitives is
entirely lost sight of. And this is much to be
regretted, since, as Callery and others have
pointed out, the scientific way of arranging the
characters would be by placing them under
their Primitives, by which means the respective
values of both the Primitives and Determinatives would be brought out in prominent relief.
Only in two Chinese dictionaries that I have
met with have any attempts been made thus to
arrange the characters, and the older of these,
and the one on which the later work was
probably framed, owes the system on which it
is composed to the experience imported from
Japan by the co-compiler, who was a native of
that country.

In the course of my remarks I have given
a few instances of the original and modern forms
of the same characters, as, for example, 馬 and
馬. But, as may readily be supposed, the
change from one to the other was not made all
at once, and Chinese books afford us instances

of six distinct styles of writing, varying in clearness from the square character used in books at the present day to the Seal and Grass or cursive characters, which are noted for their obscurity. These styles are described as the *Chuen shoo* or ' Seal character,' the *Le shoo* or ' Official character,' the *Keae shoo* or ' Model character,' the *Hing shoo* or ' Running character,' the *Tsaou shoo* or ' Grass character,' and the *Sung shoo* or 'Sung-dynasty character,' and may be illustrated by the following example, in which the character 草 *tsaou* ' herbs ' is shown written in all the six styles just specified. Seal character 艸 ; Official character 艸 ; Model character 草 ; Running character 草 ; Grass character 艸 ; and Sung character 草. But above and beyond these six styles of writing, Chinese penmen not unfrequently allow their imaginations to run riot when engaged in fanciful or ornamental pieces of caligraphy. An extraordinary specimen of this quaint taste is to be seen in the Chinese Library of the British Museum, where there is a copy of the Emperor Keenlung's Poem on Moukden, printed both in

Chinese and Manchoo in thirty-two kinds of strangely fanciful characters.

I will now pass on to the sounds of the language; and the first thing concerning them which strikes the student on becoming acquainted with his dictionary is their extreme poverty as compared with the characters. There are over 30,000 characters in the language, and these are represented to the ear by only 500 syllabic sounds. No doubt the adoption of Primitives as phonetics, as has been already described, has contributed to this result, since it provided for the due expression of those syllables then existing, but for no more. And thus, though it vastly enriched the written language—one Primitive producing as many as seventy-four derivatives—it at once put a stop to all increase in the number of the sounds. The difficulty then arose as to the way in which 500 syllables were to be made to represent in convorsation the thousands of characters in common use. And three methods have been adopted to prevent the confusion which at first sight would appear to be inevitable.

These are—1. By combining with the word
which it is desired should be understood
another, bearing a similar meaning, to dis-
tinguish it by pointing to its meaning from
other words bearing the same sound; thus, for
' to see,' it is usual to say in conversation
看 見 *kan keen,—kan* meaning ' to look at,'
and *keen* ' to see.'

2. As regards noun substantives, by placing
certain classifying words between them and the
numerals which precede them. These classifiers
bear some resemblance to our expressions *herd,
head, fleet, troop,* etc., and have a certain reference to the nature of the substantives to which
they are attached. For example, the word 把
pa ' to grasp with the hand,' is used as a
classifier to precede anything which is held in
the hand, such as a knife, a spoon, a hatchet,
etc. Instead of expressing therefore a knife
by *yih taou,* which might either mean a knife,
a small boot, or a fringe, the classifier is introduced to show which *taou* is meant, and a
speaker would say *yih pa taou,* literally ' a
grasped knife.' In like manner 開 *keen* ' a

space,' is used as a classifier for houses and
inclosures ; 棍 *kăn* ' a root,' for trees, poles,
clubs, etc., and so on.

And thirdly, by dividing the words of the
language among eight tones. These tones
partake of the nature of musical intonations,
and are divided by the Chinese into two
series, the upper and the lower, and are called
by them the upper even, the upper rising,
the upper departing, the upper entering ; the
lower even, the lower rising, the lower departing, and the lower entering. To each
character is allotted its appropriate tone, which
if wrongly rendered is liable to give an entirely
different meaning to the word from that intended by the speaker. This possibility will
be understood when it is remembered that the
thirty and odd thousand characters find expression in about 500 sounds, thus giving an
average of one sound to sixty characters, and
these figures show that at best the system of
tones is but an incomplete solution to the
difficulty, since, were this average of sixty
characters equally distributed among the full

eight tones, there would remain nearly eight
characters of each sound identical both in sound
and tone.

But, as a matter of fact, only the four tones
of the upper series are in general use, to which
sometimes the first or even tone of the lower
series is added. The even tone is, as its
name signifies, simply the ordinary tone of
voice; the rising tone gives to the voice somewhat of the effect of an interrogation; the
departing tone, of doubtful surprise; and the
entering tone, of peremptory command. These
may easily be illustrated by repeating our
negative "No," first in the ordinary tone of
conversation, secondly as an interrogation, thirdly
as expressing doubtful surprise, and fourthly
as a peremptory refusal, thus 1 No —, 2 No ╱,
3 No ╲, 4 No –. The difficulty of acquiring
a knowledge of the tones proper even to the
characters in common use is, as may be supposed, very great, and the only way to master
them is to learn them, as the children learn
them, from the lips of the natives themselves.
No study of books will give the required

knowledge. The Chinese learn them by ear
alone; and if an educated man be asked to give
the tone of an isolated character, he generally
has to repeat a phrase in which the character
occurs in order that his lips may tell his ear
the intonation proper to it.

It will be easily understood that the mistakes
and difficulties into which this intricate system
drives Chinese-speaking foreigners are often
inconvenient and sometimes dangerous. Some
years ago a petition on behalf of a Chinese
criminal was presented in person by a wealthy
Chinese merchant to the Governor and Council
of Hong Kong. A well-known Chinese scholar
undertook to interpret on the occasion, and the
Chinaman began his speech with a reference
to our *Kwai* ＼ *Kwok* or " Honourable Kingdom," as he designated England. Now the
syllable *kwai* pronounced *kwai* ／ means Devil,
and used in combination with *kwok* is an
abusive term not uncommonly applied to any
foreign country. Unfortunately the interpreter
confused the two tones, and turning indignantly
to the Governor, he reported that at the very

outset the petitioner had begun by speaking of England as " the Devil kingdom." The just anger of the Council knew no bounds, and it was only after some minutes of wild confusion that an explanation followed, which saved the Chinaman from sharing the cell of the man for whom he was pleading. To a Chinaman such a mistake would be well-nigh impossible, for the tones form integral parts of the words, and to the ear of a native the difference between *kwae* in the ascending tone, and *kwae* in the descending tone, would be as great as between *kwae* and *kwan*.

There is only one other point in connexion with the sounds of the language to which I will now refer, and that is the system which has been adopted for spelling, as it were, the various sounds. For this purpose thirty-six characters which begin with the initial consonants of the language have been chosen, and thirty-eight which end with the final sounds. In order then to indicate a desired sound, the writer takes a character of the first series which begins with the required initial, and a character of the second series which ends with the required final. These are placed together, and the initial of the first and the final of the second give the required sound. For instance, supposing a Chinaman were desirous of expressing that the sound of a certain character was *ting*, he would write the two characters 當 *tang* and 經 *king*, the first of which would give the initial *t*, and the second the final *ing*. This syllabic spelling, the initials of which are identical with the initial Sanskrit consonants, was introduced by the Buddhist missionaries in the fifth and sixth centuries, and from the time of the appearance of the Dictionary *Yuh pien*, which was published in the year 543, it has been employed in every native dictionary of the language which has since seen the light.

With a language of roots, which is devoid of inflexion or even of agglutination, in which a large number of words each play the part, under varying circumstances, of substantives, adjectives, verbs, and adverbs, it may at first sight appear that grammar must be an impossibility. But inasmuch as there are in

Chinese, as there must be in every language, certain words which, to quote Dr. Marshman, "denote things, and others which signify qualities, there must be words to express actions done, and these as done by one or many; already done, now doing, or intended to be done ; they must also be described as done absolutely or conditionally, as proper to be done, or peremptorily commanded. Further, the various circumstances of the doer, and of the subject of the action, must also be either plainly expressed or tacitly understood; hence the need of prepositions. Connecting words, too, necessarily exist in every language, as well as those which express the emotions of the mind. Thus the principles of Grammar must substantially exist in every language." And though the absence of all inflexion in Chinese places the grammar of the language on a different footing from that of the polysyllabic languages, it is yet distinctly defined by the position and connexion of the words of the sentence.

Since, when a language is spoken and understood only in the country of its birth or adoption, the study of the grammar affecting it is, as far as the natives are concerned, comparatively unimportant, we find that little attention has been paid by the Chinese to the grammar of their language. But practically the grammar, which, as I said just now, consists of rules for the construction of the sentence, has for many centuries been enforced by example, and by the censorship of the examiners at the competitive examinations. If then we observe the connexion of words which these authorities have preserved, we find that in every Chinese sentence the *subject* comes first, then the verb, which is followed by the complement direct and the complement indirect, and further that, as is the case in most of the Turanian languages, every word which defines or modifies another invariably precedes it. For instance, the adjective precedes the substantive, the adverb the verb, the genitive the word which governs it, and the preposition the word governed by it.

The importance of exactly following these

rules becomes at once apparent when we remember that often one and the same word is
capable of being used as a substantive, an
adjective, a verb, or an adverb. This is
the case also with some words in English.
We use the word *present*, for example, as a
substantive when we talk of giving a *present*;
as an adjective when we say the *present* time;
and as a verb when we say 'I *present* you.'
Cut is another word which we make use of in
the same way. We say, 'the *cut* of a sword,'
'*cut* grass,' and 'to *cut* a man down.'

A number of other instances of the same
kind might be adduced; but I will now take
a Chinese word, and show how, by varying its
position in a sentence, it changes its grammatical
value. The character 好 *hao* has for its
meanings 'to love,' 'good,' 'excellent,' 'well,'
etc.; and possibly with the intention of illustrating, as it were, these meanings by representing
the highest and purest form of natural affection,
that which exists between a mother and her
child, the inventor of the character has formed
it of two parts signifying respectively ' a

woman' and 'a son.' If, then, we meet with
it in such a connexion as this, which I have
taken from the lips of Confucius, 窺 見 室 家
之 好, *Kwei keen chĭh chia che hao,* we recognize it at once as a substantive, since, were
it an adjective, it would be followed by a
substantive; were it a verb, it would be followed
by its complement, and also because it follows
a substantive 室 家, to which is added 之, the
sign of the possessive case. . The sentence should
then be translated '*Kwei keen* to peep and see
hao the excellence or the goodness *che* of *chĭh
chia* the apartments.' In the sentence, also
from Confucius, 如 好 好 色 *Joo hao hao sĭh,*
we see by the position of the two *hao*s that the
first must be a verb, and that the second must
be an adjective, since it is followed by a substantive with which it forms the direct complement to the verb. The meaning of the sentence
then is '*Joo,* as [when] *hao*＼ we love *hao⌐ sĭh*
excellent beauty.' Again, in the modern colloquial expression 好 說 we have an example
of the use of *hao* as an adverb preceding a
verb, and the phrase is then incapable of

being translated otherwise than as 'well said,'
hao 'well,' *shwŏ* 'said.'

The number of characters which might be
treated as I have dealt with 好 is legion, and
I will not weary you with other examples.
Little has been said on the subject of this
peculiarity of the language by native grammarians, who have not done much more for
the science of grammar than to divide the
characters into 死 字 *Sze tsze* or 'Dead
words,' as they call nouns; 活 字 *Hwŏ tsze*
'Living words,' or verbs; and 虛 字 *Hsü tsze*
'Empty words,' or Particles. It is worthy of
remark that in a great many instances the tran-
sition of a character from one part of speech
to another is marked by a change of tone.
This is the case with the character *hao⁄*, of
which we have been speaking. When it stands
for the adjective 'good,' it should be pronounced in the ascending tone *hao⌐*; and when
it becomes the verb 'to love,' it is transferred
to the departing tone *hao⌐*. And in some few
cases the character suffers a change of sound as
well. 食 *shĭh*, the verb 'to eat,' is pronounced

in the entering or abrupt tone, and becomes
sze in the departing tone, when it plays the
part of a substantive meaning 'food.' In a
lecture administered to the King of Leang,
Mencius, rebuking him, says, 狗 彘 食 人 食
Kow che shih jin sze, 'Your dogs and swine
eat 'men's food.' Here you will observe the
first 食 must by the rules of position be
the verb *shih* 'to eat,' and by the same necessity this same character at the end of the
sentence must be a substantive; and the dictionaries tell us that, when this is the case, it is
pronounced *sze*. But though it is true that
a vast number of characters can be made to
serve a writer in a variety of capacities, yet
each belongs more particularly to some one part
of speech, and many are identified with that one
alone. For instance, we find that certain substantives which express things, such as *cho* 'a
table,' or *e* 'a chair,' remain fixed as substantives, and that others, if they denote actions,
are primarily verbs, and if conditions such
as 'honour,' or 'riches,' are in the first instance adjectives.

As might be expected from the nature of the
language of which this interchangeability forms
a part, Chinese admits no variation of gender,
and in this particular it agrees with the Manchu,
Mongolian, Turkish, and Finnish families of
tongues, in which, as Dr. Caldwell points out,
not only are all things which are destitute of
reason and life denoted by neuter nouns,
but no nouns whatever, not even nouns
which denote human beings, are regarded in
themselves as being masculine or feminine.
All nouns as such are neuter, or rather are
destitute of gender. " The unimaginative
Scythian reduced all things," adds the Doctor,
" whether rational or irrational, animate or
inanimate, to the same dead level, and regarded
them all as impersonal." But in every language
there are certain words the gender of which
must necessarily be distinguished, and in common
also with the people just referred to, the
Chinese prefix to such, words denoting sex.
Thus a son is spoken of as 男 子 *nan tsze*
or 'man child,' and a daughter as 女 子 *niu
tsze* or 'woman child.' In the case of animals

other characters are used. 公 *kung* 'noble,'
'superior,' is employed to denote the male, and
母 *moo* 'mother,' to indicate the female. Thus
公 獅 *kung sze* is 'a lion,' and 母 獅 *moo sze*
is 'a lioness.' With birds other characters are
considered more appropriate. Thus, the male is
described as *kung* 'martial' or 'brave,' and the
female as *tsze*, 'weak,' or 'inferior.'

As regards number, Chinese is left in an
equally indefinite condition. As a rule it is
the connexion of the words of the sentence
which determines whether a noun is in the
singular or plural. Often this is made plain
by the presence of a numeral, as in the following expression, taken from the Confucian
Analects, 三 子 者 出 'The three disciples
went out.' Here the character *san* 'three,'
indicates that *tsze* is in the plural, although it
has no inherent mark of number. Another
way of pluralizing a noun is by adding to
it one of certain words signifying 'all' or
'many.' The most common of these are 眾
chung, 諸 *choo*, 皆 *keae*, 凡 *fan*, and 等 *tǎng*.
The first four have for their meaning 'all,' and

the last, *tăng*, means 'a class.' Its use, like its meaning, is distinct from the others; they precede the noun, *tăng* always follows it, and forms with it a compound such as Animal-class for animals, Man-class for men. In colloquial Chinese the character 們 *mun* has been adopted as a sign of the plural; but its use is almost entirely confined to the personal pronouns. Thus 我 *wo* means 'I,' and 我 們 *wo mun* 'we.'

The rules of position which serve to fix the parts of speech of the words of a sentence are allowed also in great measure to regulate the cases of nouns and the moods and tenses of verbs. But this is by no means always the case. For example, the possessive case is marked by certain particles of which I shall speak presently; and although European writers on Chinese grammar have been in the habit of considering that when two substantives come together, the first is to be taken as being in the possessive case,—thus in the sentence 天 子 好 學 *Teen tsze haou heŏ*, which we should translate as 'the Son of Heaven loves learning,' *teen*, they would say, is in the possessive case,—it may be questioned whether such expressions may not be more appropriately considered as compound terms, in the same way that we treat their equivalents in English. For instance, we should never consider such an expression as ' the Chelsea-Water-Works ' to consist of a nominative and two possessive cases, as it would be parsed by these grammarians, were it turned word for word, as it might be, into Chinese. And this treatment becomes still more difficult of adoption when we find, as is often the case in Chinese, a number of substantives strung together, all of which, with the exception of the last, would then have to be considered as a succession of possessive cases. If we take, for example, one of the ordinary marks on porcelain made in China, such as 大 明 萬 曆 三 年 製 *Ta ming Wan leih san neen che*, we should be told to consider *Ta ming, Wan leih*, and *neen*, as possessive cases, and that the phrase should be translated, ' The manufacture of the third year of (the reign) Wan-leih of the Ta ming dynasty,' instead of treating it as a compound expression on the 'Chelsea-Water-Works' principle, thus 'The Ta-ming-Dynasty-Wan-leïh-third-year-manufacture.'

Besides, Chinese is by no means destitute of case-particles. In the literary and colloquial languages the possessive is expressed by suffixing respectively 之 *che* and 的 *teïh* to the substantive. Thus these particles answer exactly to the *'s* commonly used in English. 父 之 道 *Foo che taou* is 'The Way of [his] Father,' or, as we should more often say, '[His] Father's Way.' 那 個 人 的 馬 *Na ko jin teïh ma* is 'The horse of that man,' or 'That man's horse.' If we trace back the case-particle 之 *che* to its earliest use, we find that it was originally a verb, and meant 'to proceed to,' and thus, as a sign of the possessive case, it implies the sense of partition which is inherent in our 'of' and the French *de*. In some instances, by its addition to certain substantives, compound nouns of possession are formed which are capable of being used as adjectives. For example, 金 *kin* is 'gold,' and 金 之 is 'of gold,' or 'golden.' It is used also to express relation, but not as frequently as its colloquial equivalent 的 *teĭh*, which is very commonly thus employed. Such expressions as 買 馬 的 *Mai ma teĭh*, *teĭh* 'He who,' *mai* 'sells,' *ma* 'horses,' are in constant use.

With verbs of giving to and speaking to the Dative case is marked by position. The person to whom a thing is given immediately follows the verb, and the thing given comes next. The sentence 'The Prince gave to the officer some money,' is in accordance with the Chinese idiom, which would not admit the more usual English form, 'The Prince gave some money to the officer.' The Dative case, with the sense of 'for,' is marked by the use of the characters 代 *tae* 'to succeed,' 替 *te* 'to put another instead of,' and 爲 *wei* 'to be;' thus 代 人 做 事 *tae jin tso sze* 'to do something *for* a person,' 替 我 *te wo* '*for* me,' etc.

The accusative case is as a rule marked by position. But occasionally, as has been shown by M. Julien, the Particles 以 *e*, 於 *yu*, 于 *yu*, and 乎 *hoo*, are disassociated from their usual signification, and are employed simply as signs of this case.

The instrumental case is indicated by the character 以 *e* 'by' in the language of the books, and by 用 *yung* 'to use' in the colloquial. As an instance of the use of the first, I may quote the following passage from Mencius: 難 罔 以 非 其 道 *Nan wang e fei ke taou,* '(A superior man) cannot be entrapped *by* that which is contrary to right principles.'

The ablative case, having the sense of 'from,' is marked by the signs 自 *tsze,* and 由 *yew,* and in the colloquial by 從 *tsung,* as in the following examples: 自 生 民 以 來 *Tsze săng min e lae,* '*From* the birth of mankind until now;' 由 湯 至 於 武 丁 *Yew Tang che yu Woo-ting,* '*From* Tang until you arrive at Woo-ting;' 他 從 東 邊 來 了 *Ta tsung tung peen lae leaou,* 'He has come *from* the east.'

The remarks which I have made on the gender, number, and case of the substantives apply in like manner to the adjectives, and I need only refer therefore to the manner in which degrees of comparison are formed. The comparative is denoted either by certain particles meaning

'more than,' or 'beyond,' or in the colloquial
by forms of expression such as 'This man
compared with that man is good,' or, again,
'This man has not that man's goodness.' As
signs of the superlative, words such as 取 *tsuy*
'excelling,' 極 *keih* 'the highest point,' or 甚
shin 'exceeding' are employed.

In all Oriental languages the personal pronouns play a prominent part from their number
and the variety of equivalent terms, whether of
self-depreciation or of complimentary adulation,
used to express them, and in Chinese they derive
additional importance from the fact that in the
absence of all verbal inflexion, they serve to indicate the person, and in the spoken language
the number of the verb. 吾 *woo*, 爾 *urh*, and
其 *ke*, are the terms most commonly used in
classical writings to signify the first, second, and
third persons of the personal pronoun, of which
我 *wo*, 你 *ne*, and 他 *ta*, are the common colloquial equivalents. These latter have for their
plural *wo mun, ni mun, ta mun*. Quite separate
and apart from these and all their equivalents is
the character 朕 *chin*, which is reserved especially

for the Emperor, and has been the traditional imperial 'We' since the time of the three mythical Emperors to whose wisdom, energy, and foresight the greatness of China is attributed by the native historians.

But not always does the Emperor feel himself entitled to use this inherited character. In times of national misfortune he chooses to believe that his own remissness is the cause of the evils which have overtaken the country, and then it is the custom for him to designate himself *Kwa jin*, or 'Deficient man.' With his subjects the assumption of a similar humble position is habitual, and among acquaintances the place of 'I' is nearly always taken by terms by which the speaker seeks to give a complimentary importance to the person addressed at the expense of his own intellectual or social position. 'The dullard,' 'the little one,' and 'the man of low degree,' are terms most frequently used in this sense, while *nu tsae*, or 'slave,' is the self-assumed epithet adopted by ministers when addressing the Emperor. In like manner the speaker's re-

lations and personal belongings are spoken of
as 'the little,' 'the mean,' and 'the cheap.'
The respect due to age guides on the other
hand the choice of expressions employed towards
the person addressed, who, instead of being
called by the second person of the pronoun,
hears himself addressed as 'Master,' 'Old
Gentleman,' or 'Senior.' The holders of the
lower offices, such as the *Hien* or District
Magistrates, are addressed by law as *Lao ye*
or 'Old Fathers;' as they rise, they become *Ta
lao ye* 'Great Old Fathers;' and when they
reach the higher ranks, such as the Governor
of the Provinces, they are called *Ta jin* 'Great
Men.' In the same spirit it is customary to
speak of the belongings of another as being
'Worshipful,' 'Honourable,' or 'August.'

History is vague as to the date when the
Chinese adopted the numerals they at present
employ; but as we find reference to them in the
Book of History, it is fair to infer that they
were in existence before the sixth century B.C.
They are seventeen in number, and are these:
— *yih* 'one,' 二 *urh* 'two,' 三 *san* 'three,' 四

sze 'four,' 五 *woo* 'five,' 六 *lŭh* 'six,' 七 *tscĭh* 'seven,' 八 *pă* 'eight,' 九 *kew* 'nine,' 十 *shĭh* 'ten,' 百 *pĭh* 'a hundred,' 千 *tseen* 'a thousand,' 萬 *wan* 'ten thousand,' 億 *yĭh* 'one hundred thousand,' 兆 *chaou* 'a million,' 京 *keng* 'ten millions,' and 垓 *kae* 'a hundred million.' The four last are now very seldom used, the rest are hourly employed. It will be seen that there is no single numeral between ten and one hundred, and the intervening numbers are therefore formed by *shĭh* 'ten,' in combination with the lower numerals. For example, the numbers between ten and twenty are expressed by *shĭh* 'ten' with the addition of the number required. Thus 'thirteen' would be 十 三 *Shĭh san.* The figures between twenty and a hundred are denoted by 十 *shĭh* 'ten,' preceded by the other numeral, and in this way 三 十 *San shĭh* would be 'thirty.'

After the explanation, however summary, which I have given of the manner in which the number, gender, and case of nouns are clearly expressed in composition, you will not be surprised when I say that by position and the use

of particles it is possible to give expression to
all the moods and tenses of the verb. Such a
fact should not astonish us when it is recollected
that, as stated by Marshman, in the case
of certain English verbs, such as 'to cut,'
position is found equal to the task of forming
211 out of the 216 verbal variations which such
verbs undergo, and five only are formed by the
addition of terminations to the original mono-
syllable, namely 'cuttest,' 'cuts,' 'cutteth,'
'cuttedst,' and 'cutting.' As no change, not
even the lengthening of a line, or the addition
of a dot, can possibly be effected in a
Chinese character without entirely altering
its meaning, position .has to do everything
for the Chinese verb, and it accomplishes
its mission in two ways, either by stating
the time at which the action has taken place,
or is about to take place, or by prefixing or
suffixing certain words which by their several
meanings supply like information. For instance,
in the colloquial sentence 今 他 去 *kin ta keu*,
kin 'now' indicates that the action is present,
and the three characters are to be translated

'he is going.' But if we were to exchange the *kin* for 明天 *ming teen*, 'to-morrow,' the verb *keu* will be in the future tense, 'to-morrow he will go;' and if yet once again we say, *tso teen ta keu*, *tso teen* meaning 'yesterday,' the verb will then be in the past tense, and the sentence will run, 'yesterday he went.' But more frequently the present tense of the verb is not accompanied with any word to denote the time of the action, and indeed the only tense-particles employed are those which serve to explain the past and future tenses. The characters 了 *leaou* 'to complete,' and 過 *kwŏ* 'to pass over,' are the commonest of those which are suffixed to denote the first, and 將 *tseang* 'to take,' and 要 *yaou* 'to want,' are the most frequently used as prefixes to mark the second. Thus, *ta keu leaou*, or *ta keu kwŏ*, would mean 'he went,' while *ta tseang keu* or *ta yaou keu* would be 'he will go.'

In every language, as Marshman has pointed out, "it will sometimes be found necessary to indicate or declare a thing, to command an action to be performed; to express it as

desirable, obligatory, or possible; to represent
it as conditional, and to describe it in a general
way," and Chinese is no exception to this
rule. In the case of the Active and Infinitive
moods, position, which, as we have already
seen, has done so much for Chinese grammar,
is again equal to the occasion, but the Imperative, the Optative, and the Potential moods all,
although not always, have their distinctive signs.

The third person of the imperative mood, for
instance, is formed in modern Chinese by prefixing a verb meaning either 'to give,' or 'to
permit,' and answers exactly to our 'let.' 許
他 去 *heu ta keu* is 'let him go,' *heu* meaning
'to allow,' 'to permit.' The optative mood is
formed by the addition of words meaning 'to
wish,' or 'to desire,' and the potential by the
addition of words implying 'power,' 'duty,'
or 'doubt.'

It is difficult in the space of one hour to give
any idea of a language about which so little is
known, and which has so little in common with
the Indo-European tongues, as the Chinese. But
though time has prevented my entering as fully

into the subject as I could have wished, I trust the sketch I have been permitted to lay before you has served to show that by carefully following the laws of Chinese Syntax, it is possible to express in that, as exactly as in other languages, all the parts of speech in all their variety of number, gender, case, mood, tense, and person, and therefore every shade of meaning which it is possible to convey by word of mouth. The difficulties of acquiring a knowledge of Chinese have hitherto shared that exaggeration which surrounds the unknown. It is time that the language was better understood, and at this period of the world's history we cannot afford to leave unnoticed a language so ancient as to dwarf into insignificance the antiquity of western tongues, and one which is the solitary medium of communication between 400,000,000 of our fellow-men.

LECTURE II.

THE LITERATURE OF CHINA.

On Saturday last I attempted to trace the growth of the written Chinese character from its first creation as a hieroglyphic to its final development in the more modern ideophonetic form, and also the rules which govern the position of these characters in a sentence. Taking up my parable, then, at this point, my object this afternoon will be to show the use which Chinese authors have made of the characters and of the grammar to which they are subservient. It was obviously necessary to begin, as I did, with the language, before dealing with the literature, since some of the leading characteristics of the literature are, as is the case in

every tongue, plainly traceable to the structure
of the language. The words of a sentence are
as a piece of clay in the hands of a potter. If
they be soft and pliable, that is to say, if they
be capable of inflexions and of syntactical
motion, they may be moulded to express with
varying vigour and force the highest fancies
and noblest thoughts of an able writer in all
the changing beauty of poetic diction or of
rhetorical eloquence. But if on the other hand
they be destitute of inflexion, and be cramped
by inexorable laws of position, which cannot
for a moment be departed from, without a
sacrifice of sense, the result must be that the
literature of which they are the component
parts will partake to some extent of their
hard unyielding nature.

If we turn for a moment to the poetry
of ancient Greece and Rome, we find that
some of the finest effects have been produced
by the power which the inflexional nature
of those languages gave, of transposing the
position of words in a sentence so as to give
vigour and grace to the rhythm. To prove

the truth of this we have only to take some
striking passage, and compare it in the
original with a plain straightforward translation in prose. The idea is the same in both,
but how differently it appeals to the imagination of the reader! The gem is there, but it
has lost the advantage of its setting. It must
now be judged by the prosaic rule of its
intrinsic value, with no softening surroundings to add grace and brilliancy to its natural
beauty.

But the effective weapon which was thus
placed in the hands of the poets and authors of
ancient Greece and Rome has been completely
denied to Chinese writers. As I explained last
Saturday, the language is absolutely without
inflexion, and the grammar consists so entirely
of syntax, that no word can be moved out of
its determined position in a sentence, without
either changing its value, or rendering it mean-
ingloss. Thus the literature has lost much of
the variety and elegance which belongs by
nature to that of the polysyllabic languages.
And I would go beyond this and say that the

lack of that power of expression which is given by syntactical motion, has been accompanied by a blighting influence on the imaginations of Chinese authors. Other causes, to which I shall presently refer, are also to some extent responsible for this result; but in our review of the various branches of Chinese literature, we shall find that those which are most dependent for their successful development on the powers of imagination, are those which least repay attention, and that the more excellent are those which contain simple narrations of facts, or consist of the arguments of the philosopher or of the man of science.

But notwithstanding this the Chinese are eminently a literary, in the sense of a reading, people. The system of making competitive examinations the only royal road to posts of honour and emolument, and the law which throws these open to everybody who chooses to compete, have caused a wider diffusion of book learning among the Chinese than is probably to be found among any other people. As to the date when the literature first took

its rise, it is impossible to speak with any
certainty. The vicissitudes which attended the
early manuscripts and books which were collected by private individuals and in the Imperial libraries have been such as to render
the preservation of any ancient record a matter
of wonder. Constant references are found in
books to works which are said to have
existed at early dates, but of many of these
the titles are all that remain to us now.

The earliest published work on which we can
lay our hands is the "Book of Changes," the
most ancient and the most revered, because
the least understood of the nine classics. This
work first saw the light within a prison's
walls. In the year 1150 ʹ B.C. its author, Wăn
Wang, was, we are told, imprisoned for a
political offence, and sought to while away
the tedium of his confinement by tracing
out a system of general philosophy from the
eight diagrams and their sixty-four combina-
tions invented by the Emperor Fu-he. These
diagrams have been likened to the mystical
numbers of Pythagoras, and the leading idea

of Wăn Wang's system seems to have been
founded upon the Chinese notions of the creation of the world, according to which all
material things proceed from two great male
and female vivifying elements, the *Yin* and
the *Yang*, which in their turn owe their
existence to the *Tai keih*, or the first great
cause. As Sir John Davis says, this "might,
with no great impropriety, be styled a sexual
system of the universe. They, that is to say
the Chinese, maintain that when from the
union of the *Yang* and the *Yin* all existences,
both animate and inanimate, had been produced, the sexual principle was conveyed to
and became inherent in all of them. Thus
heaven, the sun, day, etc., are considered of
the male gender ; earth, the moon, night, etc.,
of the female. This notion pervades every
department of knowledge in China. It exists
in their theories of anatomy and medicine,
and is constantly referred to on every subject.
The chief divinities worshipped by the Emperor
as High Priest of the State religion are Heaven
and Earth, which in this sense appear to

answer in some degree to the οὐρανος and γη in the cosmogony of the Greeks."

The style and matter of Wăn Wang's writings were, however, so cramped and vague that Confucius among others attempted the task of elucidating their dark places. Many years the Sage spent in endeavours to make straight that which was so crooked; and the only result attained has been to add some inexplicable chapters to an incomprehensible book. But the fact that it gave rise to a system of Divination saved it from sharing the fate which, in the year 221 B.C., befell all books except those on Medicine, Divination, and Husbandry, at the hand of the Emperor Che Hwang-ti, of the Tsin Dynasty. This monarch, to whom I shall again refer, ordered, for political reasons, the destruction of all the books to be found within the Empire, except those on the subjects I have just mentioned. Fortunately, no monarch, however powerful, is able to carry out to the letter an order of so inquisitorial a nature; and the roofs of houses, the walls of dwellings, and even the beds of rivers, became the receptacles of the literary treasures of the nation until the tyranny was overpast. The works of Confucius, the "Book of History," the "Book of Odes," the "Spring and the Autumn Annals," together with the "Book of Rites," and the "Four Books" by the Disciples of the Sage and of Mencius, were all alike condemned to the flames. How all these were preserved we know not, but history tells us that, when in after years efforts were made to restore the "Book of History," twenty-eight sections out of the 100 composing the entire work were taken down from the lips of a blind man who had treasured them in his memory. One other was recovered from a young girl in the Province of Honan. And these are all which would probably have come down to us, had not a complete copy been found secreted in the wall of Confucius's house, when it was pulled down in the year 140 B.C.

This "Book of History" takes us back to about the time of Noah. It consists of a

number of Records of the Yu, Hea, Shang,
and Chow Dynasties, embracing the period
from the middle of the 24th century B.C. to
721 B.C. These, and a number of other MSS.,
attracted the attention of Confucius when he
was at the court of Chow, and selecting those
which he deemed of value, he compiled them
in a work which he called the *Shoo king* or
"Book of History."

This work, as Mr. Wells Williams says,
"contains the seeds of all things that are
valuable in the estimation of the Chinese; it is
at once the foundation of their political system,
their history and their religious rites, the basis
of their tactics, music and astronomy." For the
most part it consists of conversations between
the kings and their ministers, in which are
traced out the same patriarchal principles of
government as guide the rulers of the Empire
at the present day. "Virtue," said the minister
Yih, addressing the Emperor, "is the basis of
good government; and this consists first in
procuring for the people the things necessary
for their sustenance, such as water, fire, metals,

wood, and grain. The ruler must also think of rendering them virtuous, and of preserving them from whatever can injure life and health. When you would caution them, use gentle words, when you would correct, employ authority." "Do not be ashamed of mistakes, and thus make them crimes," was another piece of wholesome advice offered to the Emperor by his advisers, the effect of which is still observable in the outspoken confessions of official incompetence which are daily to be met with in the columns of the *Peking Gazette.*

As, in reviewing the national history, I shall treat at some length the compilation which stands next on the list of the classics—the "Book of Odes,"—I will now pass on to mention a work whose dicta have entered into the very marrow of Chinese life—I mean the Le ke, or "Book of Rites." This work is said to have been compiled by the Duke of Chow in the twelfth century B.C., since which time it has ever been the guide and rule by which Chinamen have regulated all the actions and relations of their lives. No every-day ceremony is too insigni-

ficant to escape notice, and no social and
domestic duty is considered to be beyond its
scope. From the nature of its contents, therefore, it is the work of all the classics
which has left the most palpable impression
on the manners and customs of the people.
Its rules are minutely observed at the present day, and one of the six Governing
Boards at Peking—the Board of Rites—is
entirely concerned with seeing that its precepts are carried out throughout the Empire.

Speaking of this work, Callery says with
justice, "In ceremonial is summed up the whole
soul of the Chinese, and to my mind the 'Book
of Rites' is the most exact and complete mono-
graph that this nation can give of itself to the
rest of the world. Its affections, if it has any,
are satisfied by ceremonial; its duties are ful-
filled by means of ceremonial. Its virtues and
vices are recognized by ceremonial; the natural
relations of created beings are essentially connected with ceremonial; in a word, for it ceremonial is man, the man moral, the man politic,
and the man religious, in their numberless

relations with the family, society, the state, morality and religion."

But though each and all of the classics bear to some extent the impress of Confucius, only one, the *Chun Tsew*, or "Spring and Autumn Annals," was written by him. At first sight therefore a more than usual interest attaches to this book, which is not lessened by the statements made by the Sage himself, and by contemporary scholars concerning it. "The world," says Mencius, "was fallen into decay, and right principles had dwindled away. Perverse discourses and oppressive deeds were again waxen rife. Cases were occurring of ministers who murdered their rulers, and of sons who murdered their fathers. Confucius was afraid, and made the *Chun Tsew*." As soon as it appeared, we are told that rebellious ministers quaked with fear, and undutiful sons were overcome with terror. "Its righteous decisions," said Confucius himself, "I ventured to make."

The title also of the book, we are told, was given it, because its commendations were

life-giving like spring, and its censures life-
withering like autumn. The expectant
student might therefore be excused for antici-
pating in its pages an intellectual treat. He
would look to have the history of the period
dealt with treated as a sustained narrative,
interspersed with sage reflections and deep
analyses of the characters and circumstances
of the time. He would expect to find praise
and blame distributed with a discriminating
pen, and the foul crimes of regicide and murder
denounced in impassioned outbursts of indignation. But how different is the book when we
take it up! In the words of Dr. Legge—
and I would take this opportunity of saying,
that for many of the quotations from the
classics, and for much of the information concerning them, I am indebted to that great
scholar — "Instead of a history of events
woven artistically together, we find a congeries
of the briefest possible intimations of matters in
which the court and state of Loo were more or
less concerned, extending over 242 years, without the slightest tincture of literary ability in

the composition, or the slightest indication of judicial opinion on the part of the writer. The paragraphs are always brief. Each one is designed to commemorate a fact; but whether that fact be a display of virtue calculated to command our admiration, or a deed of atrocity fitted to awaken our disgust, it can hardly be said that there is anything in the language to convey to us the shadow of an idea of the author's feeling about it. The notices, for we cannot call them narratives, are absolutely unimpassioned. A base murder and a shining act of heroism are chronicled just as the eclipses of the sun are chronicled. So and so took place: that is all. No details are given; no judgment is expressed."

The following extract from the annals of a year taken at random will be sufficient to show that Dr. Legge's remarks are well founded. " 1. In the 15th year in spring the Duke went to Tse. 2. A body of men from Tsoo invaded Seu. 3. In the 3rd month the Duke had a meeting with the Marquis of Tse and others, when they made a covenant in Mow-Kew, and then went on to Kwang. 4. Kung-sun Gaou led a force, and, with the great officers of the other princes, endeavoured to relieve Seu. 5. In summer in the 5th month the sun was eclipsed. 6. In autumn in the 7th month an army of Tse and an army of Tsoo invaded Le. 7. In the 8th month there were locusts. 8. The Duke's daughter went to her home in Tsǎng. 9. On Ke-mao, the last day of the moon, the temple of E-pih was struck by lightning. 10. In winter, a body of men from Sung invaded Tsaou," and so on page after page.

Having thus reviewed the Five Classics, I will now briefly consider the "Four Books" which, together with those just mentioned, make up the full complement of the Nine Classics. The three first of them, the *Ta-heŏ*, or "Great Learning;" the *Chung-yung*, or the "Doctrine of the Mean;" and *Lun-yu*, or "Confucian Analects," are all by the pupils and followers of the Sage; while the fourth, the *Mäng-tsze*, or the "Works of Mencius," is by a disciple of that philosopher. All these, therefore, represent the views of Confucius, and if we ask what those views point to, we find that they may be summed up in the admonition: "Walk in the trodden paths." For

as Confucius said of himself, he came not to
originate but to fulfil, and the primary object
of his teaching was to revive in a dissolute age
the purity, or supposed purity, of former generations; to quote against the roués of his day
the examples of the ancients, whom he. believed
to have been scrupulous in fulfilling the uni-
versal obligations existing between sovereign
and minister, between father and son, between
husband and wife, and between friend and
friend. Man he taught was a microcosm, and
that by striving to improve himself by acquiring knowledge, by purifying his thoughts,
by rectifying his heart, and by cultivating his
person, he would then be able to regulate his
family. When he could regulate his family,
he might then be able to govern a state; and
when he could govern a state, he might then
be trusted to rule an Empire. The Empire
was as one family; and as it was the
part of the Emperor to cherish and guard
his people as a father does a child, so it was
the duty of the people to render willing and
submissive obedience to their sovereign.

It is due to these political opinions that Confucius has become such an object of respect to both rulers and the ruled. The former see in his teaching a ready argument for the maintenance of their authority, and the people, believing that heaven has constituted for them rulers and teachers, whose duty it is to extend favour and maintain tranquillity throughout the Empire, have at the same time learnt to hold that when the ruler ceases to be a minister of God for good, he forfeits the title by which he holds the throne. Confucius was ambitious, and was a courtier, as well as philosopher, and beyond this point he avoided in any shape or way indicating the manner in which an oppressive ruler should be induced to abdicate. No such consideration influenced his disciple Mencius, who, being superior to the ordinary ambitions of man, was superior also to their common timidities, and who with much boldness of utterance freely taught that the people were the most important element in a nation, and the Sovereign was the lightest; and he did not scruple to admit the conclusion that an iniquitous ruler should be dethroned, and, if circumstances required it, that he should be put to death.

The "Confucian Analects" and the "Works of Mencius" differ in their construction from the "Great Learning" and the "Doctrine of the Mean," both of which are continuous treatises by individual authors ; whereas the two first named are records of the sayings and doings of the two Sages, compiled from memory by their faithful disciples, and somewhat resemble in construction, but at a vast interval, the plan of the Gospel narrative.

I have dwelt at some length on the classics, because, since they are the sacred books of China, it is natural to suppose that in them we may find the mainspring of the national literature. Unfortunately, to some extent this is the case, and Confucius has much to answer for, both as regards his teaching and the literary model he bequeathed to his countrymen. Instead of encouraging his disciples to think for themselves, to look into their own hearts, and to acquire that personal knowledge that enables a man to stand alone, he

led them out both by precept and example
into the dreary waste of cold formalism, in
which all individuality is lost, and all force
and originality of thinking is crushed out.
It may be said that, as far as his teachings
were concerned, he strove to suit his system
to the capacity of his audience; and that he
was successful in so doing is proved by the
fact that for twenty-two centuries his name
has been revered and his precepts have been
followed by his countrymen of whatever rank
and station in life.

As has been well observed by Wells Williams,
" If Confucius had transmitted to posterity
such works as the *Iliad*, the *De Officiis*,
or the *Dialogues of Plato*, he would no
doubt have taken a higher rank among the
commanding intellects of the world; but it
may be reasonably doubted whether his influence among his own countrymen would
have been as good or as lasting. The variety
and minuteness of his instructions for the
nurture and education of children, the stress
he lays upon filial duty, the detail of etiquette

and conduct he gives for the intercourse of all classes and ranks in society, characterize his writings from those of all philosophers in other countries, who, comparatively speaking, gave small thought to the education of the young. The " Four Books " and the "Five Classics" would not, as far as regards their intrinsic character in comparison with other productions, be considered anything more than curiosities in literature, for their antiquity and language, were it not for the incomparable influence they have exerted over so many millions of minds."

But no such apology can be offered for the example he set them in the substance and style of his writings. And we are forced to the conclusion that though a man of great force of character, he was yet strangely devoid of imagination, and that, in his blind admiration for the ancients, he constrained himself to walk humbly and passively in the paths that had been traced by others. At all events he has done his countrymen an irreparable injury. The inflexible sterility of the earliest specimens of literature might possibly have been the characteristic of a particular phase in the national mind, but Confucius helped to perpetuate it throughout all generations. As might be expected, in no class of the literature is the effect thus produced more apparent than in the commentaries on the Classics. These works are to be numbered by thousands, and, with some few exceptions, they are, as has been said of the writings of the Scribes at the time of Our Lord, cold in manner, second-hand and iterative in their very essence; with no freshness in them, no force, no fire; servile to all authority, opposed to all independence; never passing a hair's breadth beyond the carefully-watched boundary line of precedent ; full of balanced inference and orthodox hesitancy, and impossible literalism; elevating mere memory above genius, and repetition above originality.

But whatever may be the shortcoming of Confucius as a writer, the respect he felt and inculcated for letters, gave an impetus to literature. Following the example he set, men began to compile the histories of the various

States; and authors with a turn for more
original composition busied themselves with the
production of works on such arts and sciences,
including medicine, mathematics, law, and husbandry, as were known to them. It was
just as this new industry was beginning to
flourish that the Emperor Che Hwang-ti,
to whom I have already referred, an able and
ambitious prince, ascended the throne. By a
judicious mixture of force and diplomacy, he abol-
ished the Feudal States, into which the Empire
had up to his time been divided, and drew all
power and authority into his own hands.

Estimating the traditions of the past to be
almost as potent as did Confucius, and for that
very reason deeming them as dangerous to the
existence of his rule, as Confucius had considered them to be beneficial to the Empire, he
determined to break with them once and for
ever. He therefore issued an order that all
books should be burned, except those containing records of his own reign; that all who
dared to speak together about the "Book of
Odes" or the "Book of History" (harmless

subjects enough, one would think) should be
put to death, and their bodies exposed in the
market-place ; that those who should make
mention of the past, so as to blame the
present, should be put to death along with
their relatives; and that any one possessing
a book after the lapse of thirty days from
the issuing of the ordinance should be branded
and sent to labour on the Great Wall for
four years. The publication of this edict
was followed shortly afterwards by an order
for the execution of upwards of 460 scholars
who had failed to obey the mandate of the
Emperor.

Curiously enough, it was during the reign
of this uncompromising enemy to literature
that the brush pencil as at present used in
China for writing purposes was invented,
— an invention which implies that about this
time a substitute was found for the bamboo
tablets which had up to that period served the
purposes of paper. At first this new material was
a kind of closely woven silk. But this was soon
found to be as unsuitable for general purposes

from its expense, as the tablets had been from
the cumbrousness; and shortly after the establishment of the Han Dynasty, when the Decrees
of Che Hwang-ti were reversed, and every
encouragement was given by the State to men
of letters, the Marquis Tsae "invented the
manufacture of paper from the inner bark of
trees, ends of hemp, old rags, and fishing-
nets." The increased facility thus afforded for
the multiplication of books was eagerly taken
advantage of; and from the Annals of the Han
Dynasty, 206 B.C.—25 A. D., we learn that the
Imperial Library of that reigning house con-
sisted of 3123 sections on the classics, 2705 on
philosophy, 1318 of poetry, 790 on military
affairs, 2528 on mathematics, and 868 on medicine. But at the end of the second century
an insurrection, which brought the Han Dynasty
to a close, gave another check to the growing
literary taste. And though the then reigning
Emperor, in his flight from his capital at
Loyang, attempted to carry off the contents of
the Imperial Library, only half the books
reached their destination at Chang-gan, and

the remnant was shortly after given to the
flames by the successful revolutionists.

Such as had been the course of literature
up to this time, so it continued until the
close of the sixth century, when the art
of printing, which became known in Europe
nearly 900 years later, was invented in
China. A well-known Chinese Encyclopædia
tells us that on the 8th day of the 12th
month of the thirteenth year of the reign of
Wăn-ti (593 A.D.), it was ordained by a decree
that the various texts in circulation should
be collected and should be engraved on wood,
to be printed and published. Thus within a
few years of the time when St. Augustine
brought the enlightening influences of Christianity to these Isles, the art of printing—a
civilizing agency second only to Christianity—
was made known in China. But at first comparatively little use seems to have been made
of the invention; for we are told that though
it made some way during the Tang (618–907)
and the five following Dynasties (907-960), it only
arrived at its full development under the Sung

Dynasty (960–1127). It was during this last epoch that a further improvement was made in the art by the introduction of moveable types, by a blacksmith named Pe Ching. This inventor, writes M. Julien, used to take a paste of fine and glutinous clay, and make of it regular plates of the thickness of a piece of money, on which he engraved the characters. For each character he made a type, which he hardened at the fire. He then placed an iron plate on the table, and covered it with a cement composed of resin, wax, and lime. When he wanted to print, he took an iron frame divided by perpendicular threads of the same metal, and placing it on the iron plate, ranged his types in it. The plate was then held near the fire, and when the cement was sufficiently melted, a wooden board was pressed tightly upon it, so as to render the surface of the type perfectly even. This method was neither convenient nor expeditious, so says a Chinese writer, when only a few copies of a book were to be printed; but when a large number were required, it printed them off at a prodigious speed.

At this and at later periods the art of printing has been turned to no better purpose in China than to the publication of the histories of the various dynasties. Debarred both by the nature of the material at their command and by a lack of original genius from indulging in the higher branches of imaginative writing, Chinese authors have devoted themselves with untiring energy and with very considerable ability to the compilation of information concerning the physical and political features of their own and the neighbouring countries. Each dynasty has its official chronicle of these subjects, and the celebrated collection of twenty-one histories which forms a well-nigh unbroken record of the nation's annals, by contemporary authors, from the third century B.C. down to the middle of the seventeenth century, forms a notable monument of the indefatigable industry of their authors. The edition of this huge work which stands on the shelves of the Chinese Library at the British Museum is contained in sixty-six European-bound volumes of folio size. In order to facilitate the process of reference, the different histories of which it is composed, though they vary considerably in extent, are all formed on the same model. First in order come the Imperial Records, which consist of the purely political events which occurred in each reign. Then follow the Memoirs, including articles on mathematical chronology, rites, music, jurisprudence, political economy, state sacrifices, astronomy, elemental influences, geography, literature, biographies, and records of the neighbouring countries.

On all these subjects they contain a vast amount of valuable and varied information, much of which possesses considerable interest for European readers. The position which China, as a nation, has occupied and maintained through so many centuries has been such as to render her the natural depository of the annals of the kingdoms of Central and Eastern Asia. With Burmah, Cochin China, Tibet, Japan, and Corea as her vassals, with a never-ceasing relationship with the tribes of Central Asia, kept up as times and circumstances changed, now as subjects, now as allies, and now as enemies, alone unchanging in her political constitution amidst the recurring wrecks of neighbouring States, she has had the means at her command of collecting masses of ethnological information which are beyond the reach of any other people. The movements of the tribes in Central Asia, to which her policy has largely contributed, are all clearly traced in the Dynastic Annals; and it was with the view of placing the record of these within the reach of European readers that a proposal was recently made to translate, as a beginning, the History of the Han Dynasty.

Allied to these Annals are the Topographical Works of China, which for breadth of scope and for minuteness of detail are scarcely to be equalled in the literature of any other country. The most generally comprehensive of these is the *Ta Tsing yih tung chi*, which forms a geography of the Empire, together with the Chinese Districts of Mongolia and Manchuria as existing since the accession of the present Dynasty. This work, which consists of 356

books, was published at Peking in the year
1744. In it each province, each prefecture,
each department, and each district, is separately
dealt with, and are severally treated of under
the following twenty-four headings. 1. A table
of the changes which the district to be described
has undergone during the successive Dynasties
from the Han downwards. 2. Maps. 3. A list
of the distances from the various places to the
chief towns of the department. 4. Its astrono-
mical bearings. 5. Its ancient geography. 6. Its
geographical position and its notable localities.
7. The manners and customs of the inhabitants.
8. Its fortified places. 9. Its colleges and
schools. 10. The census of the population.
11. The taxes on land. 12. Its mountains and
rivers. 13. Its antiquities. 14. Its means of
defence. 15. Its bridges. 16. Its dykes. 17. Its
tombs and monuments. 18. Its temples and an-
cestral halls. 19. Its Buddhist and Taouist temples. 20. Patriotic´native officials from the time
of the Han Dynasty downwards. 21. Celebrated
men and things. 22. Illustrious women. 23. Saints
and immortals. 24. The products of the soil.

On this model distinct topographies have also been compiled, under official superintendence, of every province, every prefecture, every department, and almost every district. And not only this, but the water-ways of China, as well as the rivers of Manchuria, Mongolia, and Tibet, have all been accurately surveyed and minutely described. The narrow train of thought, however, into which the system of Chinese education has compressed the mind of the people tends to develope in them a faculty for the observation of minute details, rather than to foster the power of taking a correct comprehensive view of any wide subject. This peculiarity is observable in the class of Works of which I have been speaking; for while they are wonderfully accurate as to details, their maps and general descriptions are often vague and untrustworthy. But when we remember how only recently the very important duty of causing surveys to be made of our own Isles has been undertaken by the Government, it becomes us rather to speak with respect of the energy and wisdom shown

by the Chinese topographers, than to criticize
too closely their shortcomings.

I should be dealing unfairly by Chinese
literature were I to leave this part of my
subject without referring to the historical and
literary Encyclopædias which form so very
notable a feature in every library throughout the
country. The best known of these compilations,
and the one which may be taken as a specimen
of the class, is the *Wăn heen tung kaou,* by
Ma Twan-lin. This work has been more
largely drawn upon by European authors than
has any other Chinese book of reference, and
those who are best acquainted with it are
those who speak most highly in its praise.
"One cannot cease to admire," says Remusat,
"the depth of research which the author was
compelled to make in order to collect his
materials, the sagacity he has shown in the
arrangement of them, and the clearness and
precision with which he has presented this
multitude of objects in every light. It may
fairly be said that this excellent work is a
library in itself, and that if Chinese literature

contained nothing else, it would be worth while
to learn the language in order to read it. One
has only to choose the subject one wishes to
study, and one finds all the facts recorded and
classified, all the sources of information indicated, and all the authorities cited and dis-
cussed." "It elevates our opinion," says Wells
Williams, "of a nation whose literature can
boast of a work like this, exhibiting such
patient investigation and candid comparison of
authorities, such varied research and just dis-
crimination of what is truly important, and
so extensive a mass of facts and opinions
upon every subject of historical interest."

In point of size and importance, however,
this Encyclopædia yields place to one other,
entitled *Koo kin too shoo tseih ching,* or
" A Complete Collection of Ancient and
Modern Books." During the reign of the
Emperor Kien-lung (1735-95) it occurred
to that monarch that, in view of the gradual
alterations which were being introduced into
the texts of Works of interest and value,
it would be advisable to reprint such from the

old editions. He therefore appointed a commission, and directed them to reprint in one huge collection all such works as they might deem worthy of preservation. A complete set of copper type was cast for the undertaking, and when the Commissioners brought their labours to a close, they were able to lay before the Emperor a very palpable proof of their diligence in the shape of a compilation consisting of 6109 volumes. The contents they divided under thirty-four heads, embracing works on every subject contained in the national literature. Only a small edition was printed off in the first instance, and before long the Government, yielding to the necessities of a severe monetary crisis, ordered the copper type employed to print it to be melted down for cash. Thus only a few copies of the first edition are in existence, and it is but rarely that one finds its way into the market. It so happens, however, that one is now for sale at Peking, and it is much to be hoped that this copy of a Work which is the largest in the world, unique of its kind, and incapable of reproduction,

may, though at present fate is adverse, find
its way to the shelves of our National Library.

Time would fail me even to refer to the
immense number of biographies, and of works
on the sciences, on education, and on jurisprudence, which have from time to time
issued, and are still issuing, from the presses
in China. Nor need the literature of the
religious sects of China — the Confucianists,
the Buddhists, and the Taouists — detain me
long, since I have already introduced to your
notice the works of Confucius; and since the
great bulk of Chinese Buddhist literature is
of Indian origin. It remains, therefore, for
me to refer only to the Taouist literature, which
has its foundation in "The Sûtra of Reason
and of Virtue," by Laou-tsze, the founder of
the sect. Like Confucius, of whom he was a
contemporary, he held office at the Court of
Chow; but being less ambitious than the Sage,
he retired early from his post, and we are
told that as he passed the frontier on his way
westward, whither we know not, he placed in
the hands of the officer in charge of the

frontier guard a small volume, which embodied the results of his meditations. According to the interpretation put upon his system thus expounded by the famous commentator Choo He, it would appear to bear a strong analogy to those of the Quietists and Manicheists. " Laou-tsze's scheme of philosophy," he tells us, " consists in modesty, self-emptiness; in being void of desires, quiet and free from exertion, in being self-empty, retiring, and self-controlling in actual life." But beyond this his great object seems to have been to elucidate and develope his idea of the relations between something which he calls Taou and the Universe. To this Taou, Laou-tsze refers all things as the ultimate ideal unity of the Universe. All things originate from Taou, conform to Taou, and to Taou they at last return. Formless, it is the cause of Form. It is an eternal road; along it all beings and all things walk; but no being made it, for it is Being itself, and yet nothing. It is the path, and also the path-goers, and everything and nothing, and the cause and effect of all.

This is a sufficiently mystical foundation to allow of any superstructures, however wildly superstitious, to be based upon it. And just as the religion of Ancient Rome became incrusted and overlaid by superstitious vanities gathered from Egypt, and from wherever the Roman arms penetrated, so the teachings of Laou-tsze have been debased and disfigured in the hands of later writers, who, casting aside his profound speculations, busy themselves with the pursuit of immortality, the search after the philosopher's stone, the use of amulets, with the observance of fasts and sacrifices, rituals and charms, and the indefinite multiplication of objects of worship.

In China, as elsewhere, the first development of literary talent is found in Poetry. The Songs and Ballads which form the "Book of Odes," to which I have already referred, date back to a time long antecedent to the production of any works of which we have knowledge. In those early days, before China was China, the then Empire was divided into a number of feudal states, all of which, however, acknow-

ledged fealty to the ruling Sovereign, at
whose Court were a number of music-masters
and historiographers, whose duty it was to
collect and set to music the songs of the
people, and to preserve the historical records
of the Empire. In strict imitation of the
surroundings of their liege Lord, the feudatory
Princes numbered among their retinues officers
of like position, and professing similar func-
tions. At stated intervals these Princes, accompanied by their followings, were in the habit
of meeting the King at certain recognized
places to take orders for the future and to
receive credit or blame as the case might be for
their past conduct. On such occasions the music-
masters would carry with them the Ballads and
Songs collected in their principalities, and
present them to their Superior at the Royal
Court. These he would collect and classify,
reminding one of Queen Elizabeth's Minister,
who, according to the Spectator, "had all
manner of books and ballads brought to
him, of what kind soever, and took great
notice how much they took with the people;

upon which he would, and certainly might
very well judge of their present dispositions,
and of the most proper way of applying them
according to his own purposes." Thus it
happened, that at the time of Confucius there
existed an official collection of some 3000 songs.
On these the Sage set to work, and, in the words
of the historian Sze-ma Tseen, "he rejected
those which were only repetitions of others,
and selected those which would be serviceable
for the inculcation of propriety and righteous-
ness." Such he arranged to the number of 311
under four heads, namely, *National Airs, the
Lesser and Greater Eulogies,* and the *Songs of
Homage,* and gave the title of *She king,* or
" Book of Odes," to the collection.

If we can imagine ourselves seated in the
study of the royal minister, searching with
him into the Ballads ⋅ thus laid before us
for an indication of the temper and mind
of the people among whom they had had
their birth, we should be inclined to con-
gratulate him on the easy task entrusted to
him of governing such a population. Through

7

most of them there breathes a quiet calm and patriarchal simplicity of thought and life. There are few sounds of war, little tumult of the camp, but, on the contrary, a spirit of peaceful repose, of family love and of religious feeling. We have brought before the mind's eye the lowly cottage, where dwell a family united by the bonds of affection and of duty. Their food is the produce of the soil and the spoils of the chase. The highest ambition of the men is to excel as archers and charioteers, and their religious worship is the same as that which, untainted by Buddhism or any other form of philosophical teaching, is now practised at the Imperial Temples of Heaven and Earth, by the Emperor only as High Priest. Their wives are objects of affection and respect, and though in one song we find the belief expressed that "a wise woman will ruin a city," yet there seems to have been abundance of regard for honest housewives who did their duty, who shared the toil of their husbands, and enjoyed with them the simple pleasures within their reach.

It is true that now and again we meet with traces of scenes of revelry bordering on licentiousness; but their idyllic surroundings, and the absence of all violence, deprive the most dissolute descriptions of all vulgarity and coarseness. More serious by far are the wailing complaints of misrule and tyranny under which the subjects of certain princes groan. But even here there are no signs of insubordination or tumult; the remedy which suggests itself to a people, patient and long-suffering to a degree, is to emigrate beyond the reach of the tyrant, not to rise in rebellion against him. In the following lines, for instance, the writer begs his friends to fly with him from the oppression and misery prevailing in his native State, which he likens to the North wind and thickly falling snow:

> "Cold blows the North wind;
>   Thickly falls the snow.
> Oh come all ye that love me,
>   Let 's join hands and go.
> Can we any longer stay,
> Victims to this dire dismay?"

Foxes and crows were looked upon as creatures
of evil omen, and so, giving play to his imagination, he tells us that the only variations
noticeable in the monotony of the present dis-
tress were these prognostics of future evil, in
these words,

> " Nought red is seen but foxes,
>   Nor aught else black but crows,
> Oh come all ye that love me,
>   Let 's fly before our foes.
> Can we any longer. stay,
>   Victims to this dire dismay ? "

Though the style and diction of these
songs are of the simplest description, yet
through some of them there runs a rich vein
of sentiment, and in forming a judgment on
them it is necessary to remember that they
are not studied poems, but simply what
they profess to be, songs of the people.
Like all political ballads also, many of them
refer to contemporary events about which we
know next to nothing; and in estimating their
merits, therefore, we are much in the same posi-

tion as that in which a Chinaman would be
placed, who, in the year of our Lord 3000,
might criticize the poetical squib in last week's
" Punch " on the Derby, without ever having
heard of that great cockney festival. We are
therefore much in the hands of the com-
mentators, and they tell us that the following
song is intended to depict a rural scene, in
which an industrious wife impresses on her
husband the necessity of early rising, and en-
courages him to make virtuous and respectable
acquaintances :

" Get up, husband, here's the day ! "
" Not yet, wife, the dawn's still grey."
" Get up, Sir, and on the right
   See the morning star shines bright.
   Shake off slumber, and prepare
   Ducks and geese to shoot and snare.

" All your darts and line may kill
   I will dress for you with skill.
   Thus, a blithesome hour we'll pass,
   Brightened by a cheerful glass ;
   While your lute its aid imparts
   To gratify and soothe our hearts.

"On all whom you may wish to know
I'll girdle ornaments bestow;
And girdle ornaments I'll send
To any one who calls you friend;
With him whose love for you 's abiding
My girdle ornaments dividing."

> (*The Book of Odes*, Pt. I. Bk. vii. Ode 8.)

One other I will quote, taken from the Songs of Homage, or Hymns which were sung either by or before the Emperor when he sacrificed as High Priest to God. We are told that this one was sung by King Seuen on the occasion of a great drought in the eighth century before Christ. In it he expostulates with God for bringing this misery upon him, and expresses his belief that he had a right to expect succour instead of disaster from the Most High.

Brightly resplendent in the sky revolved
The milky way.
                    The monarch cried, Alas!
What crime is ours, that Heaven thus sends on us
Death and Disorder, that with blow on blow
Famine attacks us?

Surely I have grudged
To God no victims; all our store is spent
Of tokens. Why is it I am not heard?—
Rages the drought. The hills are parched, and dry
The streams. The demon of the drought
Destroys like one who scatters fiery flames.
Terrified by the burning heat my heart,
My mourning heart, seems all consumed with fire.
The many dukes and ministers of the past
Pay me no heed.
O God! from Thy great Heaven
Send me permission to withdraw myself
Into seclusion.
Fearful is the drought.
I hesitate, I dread to go away.
Why has this drought been sent upon my land?
No cause for it know I. Full early rose
My prayers for a good year; not late was I
In off'ring sacrifice unto the Lords
Of the four quarters and the land.
Afar
In the high Heaven God listens not. And yet
Surely a reverent man as I have been
To all intelligent Spirits should not be
The victim of their overwhelming wrath.

(*The Book of Odes*, Pt. 111. Bk. 111. Ode 4.)

Such is the poetry of the Book of Odes,

and such we should have expected to find
it, since the earliest specimens of poetry in
every land partake of a simple and religious
nature, are crude in their measure, and are
wanting in that harmony which is begotten
of study and cultivation. The Chinese say
of poetry that the Book of Odes may be
likened to its roots, that during the Han
and Wei Dynasties it burst into foliage, and
that during the Tang Dynasty (620-907) it
came into full bloom. Certainly the change
that came over it after the time of Confucius
is very marked. Instead of the peaceful Odes
of his day, we find pieces reflecting the un-
settled condition of political and social affairs.
Songs breathing fire and sword, mingled with
wild fancies, the offspring of Taouist teaching, have taken the place of the domestic
ballads of the Book of Odes. The simple
monotheistic belief of the early Chinese is
exchanged for a superstitious faith in a host
of Gods and Goddesses, who haunt every hill,
and dance in every glade. As a specimen of
the Poetry of this period, I may quote the

following " Lament of a Soldier on a Campaign,"
by Sun Tsze-king, of the Wei Dynasty.

On the hilly way blows the morning breeze; the
 Autumn shrubs are veiled in mist and rain.
The whole city escorts us far on our way, providing us
 with rations for a thousand *li*.
Their very worst have the three Fates done. Ah me!
 how can I be saved. There is nought more
 bitter than an early death. Do not the Gods desire
 to gain perpetual youth?
As Sorrow and Happiness, so are Fortune and Misfortune intermingled. Heaven and Earth are the
 moulds in which we are formed, and in them is
 there nothing which does not bear significance.
Far into the future looks the sage, early striving to
 avert calamity. But who can examine his own
 heart, scrutinize it by the light of heaven, regulate
 it for his present life, and preserve it for the
 old age which is to come?
Longer grows the distance from what I have left
 behind me: my trouble is greater than I can bear.

With other Poets this new phase of belief
encouraged a contempt for life, and an uncertainty of all beyond it; and these during
the first two centuries gave vent to their

indifference in Odes advocating the Epicurean philosophy, " Let us eat and drink, for to-morrow we die." Eight short Dynasties, times of confusion and disorder, followed after the Han Dynasties (206 B.C.–221 A.D.) ; and then came the Tang Dynasty (620–907), a period which is looked back upon as being the golden age of literature, as indeed it was in every field which marks a nation's greatness. It was during this epoch that Imperial armies occupied Bokhara and Samarcand, that the Buddhist traveller Heuen-tsang made his way to India, and to every spot rendered sacred by the presence of Buddha, and that the softening influences of Christianity were introduced by the Nestorians into the very heart of the Empire. It was a time of prosperity and peace. Literature flourished, and skill and art were employed to soften and add harmony to the national ·poetry. The four syllables, of which nearly all the lines in the Book of Odes were composed, were exchanged for five and seven. The subjects also partook of the change. Le Tae-pïh, the greatest poet

of his time, tuned his lyre to notes on the
pleasures of wine and of beauty, which would
have done honour to Anacreon. Evening feasts
amid the parterres of gardens rich with the
bloom of a thousand flowers furnished themes
upon which he and his imitators were never
tired of dilating. Such sonnets are sometimes
pretty, and occasionally the ideas they contain
are striking; but the disadvantages of the
language and of education weigh heavily upon
their authors, and they seldom rise beyond
the level of the merest mediocrity. The following is taken from the writings of the poet
I have just mentioned, and is translated
lineatim et verbatim :—

A Solitary Carouse on a Day in Spring.

The east wind fans a gentle breeze,
The streams and trees glory in the brightness of the
         Spring,
The bright sun illuminates the green shrubs,
And the falling flowers are scattered and fly away.
The solitary cloud retreats to the hollow hill,
The birds return to their leafy haunts.

Every being has a refuge whither he may turn,
I alone have nothing to which to cling.
So seated opposite the moon shining o'er the cliff,
I drink and sing to the fragrant blossoms.

Of epic poetry the Chinese know nothing, and this need not surprise us when we remember how entirely that style of writing was an importation from Greece into Western Europe; and Voltaire tells us, that when he was thinking of publishing the Henriade, he consulted a friend on the subject, who recommended him to give up the undertaking,—"for," said he, "the French have not epic heads." Neither have the Chinese. A sustained effort of imagination is difficult to them, and the strict laws of rhyme and metre which hamper the poet would make a lengthened poem in Chinese the work of a lifetime. It is probably due to this cause that the literature shows no instance of real dramatic poetry. Their dramas abound with short lyrical pieces, which are introduced to break the monotony of the dialogue; but dramas in verse are unknown, except in the case of low plays written in vulgar rhythm. As, however, love for the drama is one of the most noticeable features of the Chinese character, every encouragement has been given to playwrights, and this branch of literature is therefore well supplied both as regards matter and bulk. The most celebrated plays are contained in a collection entitled "The Hundred Plays of the Yuen Dynasty," many of which have been translated into European languages, and one of which, *The Orphan of Chaou,* served as the groundwork of Voltaire's tragedy, "L'Orphelin de la Chine." Their dramas are divided in the playbooks into acts, generally four or five; but as there is an absence of all scenery, and as the dresses are never changed during the piece, the acting is as a rule continuous throughout without break or interval. The stage directions are given in their books as in ours, but not with the same minuteness. "Enter" and "Exit" are expressed by "Ascend" and "Descend," and "Aside" by "Turn the back and say." By the rules of the Chinese, as was the case also in the Greek, drama, only two players are allowed to have possession of the stage at any one time. This, and the absence of all scenery, obliges the dramatists to put in the mouths of the actors long pieces of spoken narrative, much after the manner of the prologue in the Plays of Euripides, which appear tame and heavy to a European spectator accustomed to have the plot and locality explained by dialogue and scenery. The plots are for the most part simply and well sustained. The unities, though sometimes observed, are more often disregarded, especially that of place, the characters being frequently sent to different parts of the country in the same act, and are made to inform the audience of their whereabouts by the simple expedient of walking up and down the stage, and exclaiming, "Now I am at such and such a place," or "at such and such a house." The acting, generally speaking, is good. The Chinese are actors by nature, and are no doubt a good deal improved by their inherent cunning and want of sincerity, which make them quick of observation and fertile in resource, and in every-day life enable them easily to catch the tone of those with whom they associate, and on the stage to assume the characters they wish to represent.

The theatre is in China, as it was in Greece, national and religious. It is under the direct control of the law, and is closed by Imperial edict during all periods of public mourning, while at the same time it plays a prominent part at all the yearly religious festivals. In order to give some idea of the substance and plot of a Chinese drama, I will quote from Sir John Davis's "China" an abstract of a play, which he has translated and published at full length, entitled "The Heir in Old Age." This piece serves, as is observed by the translator, to illustrate the consequences which the Chinese attach to the due performance of the oblations at the tombs of departed ancestors, and also the true relation of the handmaid to the legitimate wife. The *dramatis personæ* are, he says, "made up entirely of the members of a family in the middle class of life, consisting of a rich old man, his wife, a handmaid, his nephew, his son-in-law, and his daughter."

The old man, having no son to console him in his age, and to perform the obsequies at his tomb, had, like the Jewish Patriarch, taken a handmaid, whose pregnancy is announced at the opening of the play, in which the old man commences with saying, "I am a man of Tung-ping Foo, etc." In order to obtain from Heaven a son, instead of a daughter, he makes a sacrifice of sundry debts due to him, by burning the bonds, and this propitiatory holocaust serves at the same time to quiet some scruples of conscience as to the mode in which part of his money had been acquired. He then delivers over his affairs to his wife and his married daughter, dismissing his nephew (a deceased brother's son) with a hundred pieces of silver to seek his fortune, as he had been subjected at home to the persecution of the wife. This done, the old man sets out for his estate in the country, recommending the mother of his expected son to the humane treatment of the family, and with the hope of receiving from them speedy congratulations on the birth of a son.

The son-in-law now betrays to the daughter his disappointment at the expected birth, since, if it prove a girl, they shall lose half the family property, and if a son, the whole. His wife quiets him by a hint how easily the handmaid may be got rid of, and the old man persuaded that she had suddenly disappeared; and shortly afterwards both the son-in-law and the audience are left to infer that she had actually contrived to make away with her. In the mean time the old man waits the result in great anxiety; his family appear in succession to console him for the loss of his hopes. In the bitterness of his disappointment, he bursts into tears, and expresses his suspicions of foul play. He then attributes his misfortunes to his former thirst for gain, resolves to fast for seven days, and to bestow alms publicly at a neighbouring temple, in the hope that the object of his charity may treat him as a father. Among the beggars at the temple, his nephew appears in the most hopeless state of poverty, being reduced to take up his

lodgings under the furnace of a pottery;
he is insulted by the son-in-law, and re-
proached by the old wife; but his uncle,
moved with compassion, contrives to give him
a little money, and earnestly advises him to
be punctual in visiting the tombs of his
family at the approaching spring, assuring
him that a due attention to those sacred
rites must ultimately lead to prosperity. It is
on the importance attached to the sepulchral
ceremonies that the whole drama is made to
turn.

The nephew accordingly appears at the tombs,
performs his oblations as well as his poverty
will admit, and invokes the shades of his ancestors to grant him their protection. He no
sooner departs than the old man appears with
his wife, expressing their indignation that their
own daughter and son-in-law had neglected to
come with the customary offerings. They
observe, from the appearances at the sepulchre,
that their nephew must have been there. The
scene at the tombs, and the reflections of the
old man thereon, have considerable interest;

he reasons with his wife, and convinces her that the nephew is nearer in blood and more worthy than the son-in-law; she relents, and expresses a wish to make him reparation; he appears, and a reconciliation takes place, and he is received back into the family. The son-in-law and daughter now enter with a great bustle and a procession, to perform the ceremonies, but are received with bitter reproaches for their tardy piety and ingratitude, and forbidden to enter the doors again.

On the old man's birthday, however, they claim permission to pay their respects, when, to the boundless surprise and joy of the father, his daughter presents him with the long-lost handmaid and child, both of whom, it appears, had been secreted by the daughter, unknown to her jealous husband, who supposed they were otherwise disposed of. The daughter is taken back, and the old man divides his money in three equal shares, between her, his nephew, and his newly-found son; the play concluding with expressions of joy and gratitude that the venerable hero of the piece had obtained an "heir in his old age."

This play furnishes us with a very good type of Chinese plays in general. The incidents are true to life, but they have no psychological interest about them. There is no delineation of character in it, and there is nothing in the plot to make it more appropriate for the groundwork of a play than for that of a novel. In the works of fiction we. are treated only to the same crude narration of facts, without any just representation of nature. Exaggerated sentiments, which always precede correct reasoning and refined simplicity, fill the pages of their works of fiction, rendering them favourites only with those who are taught to judge of them according to their own standard of taste. Of the characters portrayed, we have to judge only from actions attributed to them, which are strung together with no connecting links, except those supplied by the iteration of details, which are wearisome to a degree. Several novels have been translated into English by Sir John Davis and others ; but, from the causes I have described, few have attracted any public interest. Some of their shorter tales, being to a great extent purged of the cumbrous repetitions common to larger works, are better capable of translation, and the novelty of many of the situations and incidents serves to keep alive the attention of the reader. Unfortunately the tone of most Chinese novels is not such as to afford any palliation for the dreariness of their contents. If Chinese novelists are to be believed, virtue in women and honour in men are to be found only in a few rarely-gifted individuals, and this has been so constantly insisted on, that it appears to have become one of those beliefs which have been the means of their own justification.

If then, having considered the past and present literature of China, we cast a glance into the future, the prospect is not encouraging. Already every subject within the scope of Chinese authors has been largely treated of and infinitely elaborated. Every grain of wheat has long ago been beaten out of it, and any further labour expended upon it can but be only as thrashing out straw. The only hope for the future of the literature is that afforded by the importation of foreign knowledge and experience into the country. For many years these can only be introduced in the shape of translations of books. But the time will come when Chinese authors will think for themselves; and when that period arrives, they will learn to estimate their present loudly-vaunted literature at its true value.

STEPHEN AUSTIN AND SONS, PRINTERS, HERTFORD.